celtic mysism

celtic mysticism

WALKING WITH THE GODS: A SPIRITUAL GUIDE

anthony duncan

southwater

This edition is published by Southwater

Southwater is an imprint of
Anness Publishing Limited
Hermes House
88–89 Blackfriars Road
London SE1 8HA
tel 020 7401 2077
fax 020 7633 9499

Distributed in the UK by
The Manning Partnership
251–253 London Road East
Batheaston
Bath BA1 7RL
tel 01225 852 727
fax 01225 852 852

Distributed in the USA by
Anness Publishing Inc.
Suite 504
27 West 20th Street
New York NY 10011
tel 212 807 6739
fax 212 807 6813

Distributed in Australia by
Sandstone Publishing
Unit 1, 350 Norton Street
Leichhardt
New South Wales 2040
tel 02 9560 7888
fax 02 9560 7488

Publisher: Joanna Lorenz, *Senior Editor:* Joanne Rippin
Special photography: Don Last, *Designer:* Nigel Partridge
Production Controller: Yolande Denny, *Reader:* Richard McGinlay

1 3 5 7 9 10 8 6 4 2

The publishers would like to thank the following picture libraries and photographers for the
use of their pictures in the book: Ancient Art & Architecture: 6t; 7tl; 13t; 36. AKG Photo: 1;
6br; 18t; 20tl; 21tr; 30; 35tl; 39tl; 46bl; 47bl; 48; 49; 50bl; 54; 56; 57tl; 58t; 62tr; 63tl. The Art
Archive: 12; 18bl. Mary Evans Picture Library: 10; 11tl, tr; 13br; 14bl, r; 15; 16; 17tl, br; 26tl,
tr, bl; 32bl, tr; 33tl, br; 40bl, tr; 64tr. Fine Art Photographic: 19; 26br; 51t; 55br; 60bl; 62bl;
63br. Fortean Picture Library: 2; 5; 25b; 31tl, tr; 34tr; 38bl; 39br; 43; 50br; 53; 55tl; 58bl; 59tr,
b; 61t; 64bl. Getty Stone Images: 7tr; 20bl, tr; 23tr; 23b; 45br; 51bl; 56tr; 61bl. Images Colour
Library: 23tr; 44; 45tl; 47tr; 61br. Elizabeth Rees: 38br. Mick Sharp Photography: 4; 29; 37tl,
br; 57br; 59tl; 60tr. Werner Forman Archive: 3; 9; 21br; 34bl; 35tr; 46tr, br.

CONTENTS

Introduction 6

Chapter One:

The Importance of Myth 8

Chapter Two:

The Fulfilment of Celtic Paganism 28

Chapter Three:

Mysticism: an Attitude of Mind

and Heart 42

Chapter Four:

True Mysticism 52

The Festivals of the Celtic Year 62

Index 64

INTRODUCTION

—

The Celtic approach to life is a holistic one, acknowledging the cyclic nature of
existence and making no false distinctions between the sacred and the secular.
The whole of creation is the transfigured image of its creator, and earth and heaven,
or the physical and the spiritual, are parts of a unity.

Today, people of Celtic descent in Europe are concentrated on its western shores. They live chiefly in Brittany, Cornwall, Wales, Scotland, the Isle of Man and Ireland. However, the Celts dominated much of Western Europe for some fifteen hundred years before Christ. They occupied an area that stretched from the Black Sea, along the length of the Danube basin and into both France and Spain. Their origins lie in the late Bronze Age but they are essentially an Iron Age people and were known to their neighbours, the Greeks, as Keltoi, and to the Romans as Celtae or Galli. Celts also ventured as far as Asia Minor and these people, called the Galatae (or Galatians), are referred to in the New Testament.

Celtic culture was heroic and tribal. They were formidable warriors and expert charioteers. The Celts also excelled in metallurgy and their artistic skills were lavished on ornaments, brooches, decorations for horse-harnesses, weapons and shields and what we would now recognize as luxury goods. They were vigorous traders and their tribal society was evidently advanced, but they left no first-hand written records. The ancient Celts relied on oral accounts and trained memories to pass on their history. Their myths and legends were eventually written down by Celtic Christian monks from the fifth century onwards, when the old Celtic civilization was nearing its end.

ABOVE: Celtic brooch. 5th century BC.

BELOW: Celtic helmet fashioned in bronze, iron, enamel and gold. 4th century BC.

BELOW: The Tara brooch. 8th century.

RIGHT: Ballinskelligs Bay, Co Kerry, Ireland.

WHO WERE THE CELTS?

The Celts migrated westwards into Britain during the first millennium BC, probably intermarrying with earlier inhabitants. The whole of present-day England and Wales was peopled by what are known as Brythonic-speaking Celts, the language from which Welsh, Cornish and Breton derive. A completely different branch of the Celtic race invaded Ireland, from Spain, in about the fourth century BC, displacing the earlier inhabitants by war or by intermarriage. These were Gaelic speakers, from whose language Irish, Scots Gaelic and Manx derive.

Until the rise of Roman power, the Celts were a force to be reckoned with and Rome itself had been sacked by them in 385BC. This was not to last and Julius Caesar gained victory between 59 and 48BC over the Celtic tribes living in Gaul (present-day France). Although many Celts were incorporated into the Roman empire, their religion and mythology survived largely intact until Rome adopted Christianity in the fourth century AD.

Perhaps the most unique aspect of the Celtic inheritance is their mystic approach to life. At the centre of a Celt's spirituality was an attitude that saw no separation between the gods and man, or between this world and the next, or between the past and the present. An illustration of this ability to fuse diverse elements is the way the Celts adopted a version of the Christian faith, that was uniquely holistic and which grew organically from what had gone before. This holistic approach is one that holds more resonance today than ever before and is an integral part of what we refer to as Celtic mysticism.

CHAPTER ONE

THE IMPORTANCE OF MYTH

The Celts had an oral tradition rooted in myth, which was both poetic and dramatic. Myth is poetry, it articulates what flat, academic historical prose can never express for it comes from the hearts of a people rather than from their heads.

THE OTHERWORLD

The spiritual world of pagan Celtic understanding is very much earthbound. It is the home of a pantheon of archetypes – and the embodiments of basic human dynamics – in which the traditions of earlier cultures were probably assimilated. The Otherworld is not a dismal abode of the dead but a glittering world, close to – and acting upon – reality.

EARTH, STARS AND ANNWN

Ancient peoples, worldwide, were aware of the procession of the equinoxes, whereby the Earth's axis gradually shifts from one constellation to another. At about the time of the Celtic occupation of Britain, this alignment was in the process of change from the constellation of Draco, the Dragon, to that

of Ursa Minor, the Little Bear. The Earth's axis extended to the heavenly Pole Star so that its influence penetrated the Goddess, Mother Earth herself. The Pole star in Draco was Alpha Draconis. In Ursa Minor it was Polaris. It was believed then that the ruling constellation was reflected in the deeds of men and women and in the earliest sources of the Arthurian myths, Arthur's name is derived from the Welsh Arth, meaning "Bear". His mythological father was Uther Pendraig (Pendragon, "chief of the dragon"). In Celtic mythology, the Bear therefore succeeded the Dragon.

ANNWN, THE CELTIC HEAVEN

In Celtic mythology heaven was not merely a place that the dead inhabited. Their heaven, called Annwn, in the Celtic world-view, is a reality that is experienced by the sensitive. It has doors and gateways to this world, through which seers and bards can pass on spirit-flights or journeys of the soul. Intrepid heroes may find such gateways, which are often through water,

LEFT: Arthur receives the sword Excalibur from the Lady of the Lake, a goddess from the Otherworld.

ABOVE: The bean-sidhe, the fairy woman.

RIGHT: At his time of death Arthur is taken, by water, out of this world and into another.

across narrow bridges or beneath mounds. On the eve of Samhain, 31 October, the Celtic festival of the dead, the gateways to the Otherworld are said to open. One of the most potent places in Celtic mythology is Llyn Tegid, or Lake Bala, in Wales. There, gods and goddesses dwell underwater, or on an invisible island. It was from the Lady of the Lake that Arthur received his sword. She was said to be the foster-mother of Launcelot of the Lake. She named and armed him and he walked to dry land on a sword blade.

There are many stories of those who entered the Otherworld to find it a paradise where time and space do strange things. Nera spent three days with the *sidhe* (or fairies) and returned to find that no time had passed. The little fairy mound contained a vast community, with its dwellings and lands. Bran Mac Feba returned from his voyage to the Otherwordly Islands of the West to discover that he was now the stuff of ancient legend. As one of his crewmen stepped ashore he crumbled to dust. Maelduin crossed a crystal bridge to visit the Isle of Women. The fairy women of the Otherworld, known as the *bean-sidhe* (or banshee), are royally attired and bear wounded heroes away to heal them, just as Morgana bore the dying Arthur away over the water to Avalon where he would be healed and

MYTHOLOGICAL ORIGINS

—

The Celts held the spoken word in the highest regard, and their myths, legends and traditions were transmitted orally. Although they had no specific creation myth, the legend that human beings were descended from trees, which were also the source of poetry, reflects the deep-seated Celtic sense of interconnection with the natural world.

THE IRISH CELTS

There is a well-known mythological sequence giving the story of how the land of Ireland was populated. The first inhabitants, just three men and 51 women, all perished in the great flood of the Old Testament. All that is except for one man, Fintan, who survived by changing himself first into a salmon that swam through the waters, then into a hawk so that he could watch the mountains reappear as the flood drained away.

Invaders then sailed in from the West but fell to fighting among themselves. Their numbers were further diminished when a plague overcame them. Nine survivors of a fleet, lost in the ocean, then settled in Ireland and ruled for many centuries until they were overcome by evil spirits and were either killed or fled. One chief, called Britan, fled to the mainland that now

LEFT: A nineteenth-century artist's impression of an elaborately dressed Arch Druid.

bears his name. Others fled to Ancient Greece and eventually returned: among them were the Fir Bolg (possibly Belgae, Celts from Northern France) who, with others, created the five provinces of Ireland. The next invaders were the Tuatha de Danaan, the people of the goddess Danu. They came flying through the air and landed in Ireland on the first day of May.

The magical powers of the Tuatha de Danaan were able to overcome the magic of the evil spirits who lived on an island, and whose demon-king was called Balor. Balor was slain by the spear of Lugh, the warrior-god of the Tuatha, who had first to avenge the death of his father, Kian, who had been killed by the three sons of Turenn. This he did by setting the brothers the task of obtaining the magical weapons needed to defeat Balor.

The Tuatha ruled Ireland until a new race of tall and beautiful people – the Celts – arrived from Spain. They and the Tuatha agreed to divide Ireland between them. The Tuatha would live beneath the ground and the Celts would live above it, and so it has been to this very day.

LEFT: Irish ollamh and bard.

or women and were shamans, mediators, knowers and keepers of wisdom. Like the bards, all their lore was memorized and passed down verbally. They acted as both priests and judges.

BARDS AND DRUIDS

Next to the king, or warlord, the most important figures in Celtic society were the druid and the bard or poet. The attainment of the seven grades of a bard lasted twelve years, of which the first six were devoted to memorizing stories, learning grammar, law and what was known as the Secret Language of Poets. In his seventh year he was called anruth or "noble stream". In the last three years he became an ollamh, or doctor, and by the time he had finished his training he knew 100 poems of a type restricted to ollamhs, 120 orations, the Four Arts of Poetry and 350 stories.

The druids (*drui* in Irish, *derwydd* in Welsh) were seers, with an intimate knowledge of the natural world, who walked between the outer world and Annwn, the Otherworld. They could be either men

RIGHT: A druid performs the ceremonial cutting of the sacred plant mistletoe.

heroes and heroines

In every culture, legends evolve about heroes and heroines who are the archetypal characters of the age, the tribe or the race. The Celtic heroes were role-models for the Celtic warrior. They were hard-fighting, hard-drinking, hot-tempered, lustful and boastful, but also passionate, brave and idealistic.

LEGENDARY WARRIORS

Finn MacCool, who built the Giants' Causeway for his convenience, and Cuchulainn, the champion warrior of Ulster, who filled his chariot with the heads of his enemies, were both larger-than-life

ABOVE: *Cuchulainn carries Ferdiad across the river.*

LEFT: *Cuchulainn rides into battle.*

rowdies. Gilla Stag-shank could clear three hundred acres in one leap, Henbeddestr could outrun men on horseback and Gwaddn Osol could level a mountain by standing on it.

The authority of the Welsh chieftain, Pwyll, even extended into the Otherworld. In order to settle a debt of honour, he changed places for a year with Arawn, king of Annwn, and succeeded in killing a rival who had to be vanquished with a single blow. The code of honour Pwyll followed links him with the heroic figure of King Arthur and the numerous legends of the Round Table which later became popular medieval romances.

PEERLESS WOMEN

Celtic heroes often learned the arts of war from warrior women and it was the mother who would name and arm the warrior. Cuchulainn, for example, was sent to Skye to learn the arts of war from Scathach, a warrior goddess, and to learn the arts of love from her daughter Uathach.

The heroines of Celtic myths enjoyed power and commanded armies in their own right, as did the historical Queen Boudicea, who led a revolt against Roman rule in first-century Britain. Queen Maeve of Connacht was believed to hold the kingdom's sovereignty in her person, and no king could reign there unless he was married to her. Her most famous action was the invasion of Ulster, when her forces captured the great brown bull of Cuailgne in

ABOVE: Maeve the Warrior Queen.

the war against Cuchulainn. Emer, Cuchulainn's wife, was said to be blessed with the six gifts of womanhood: beauty, chastity, wisdom, sweet speech, song and needlecraft. But she also demanded that Cuchulainn should improve his fighting skills and prove himself before she would marry him.

THE MYTHS AND THE SORROWS

*There is both joy and sorrow in Celtic myths which reflect the reality of life
and the Celt is nothing if not a realist.*

A thread of tragedy runs through Celtic mythology: there are many stories of outcasts, doomed lovers and lost children. The love-story of Diarmid and Grainne ends with Diarmid being killed by a wild boar, while both Tristan and Isolt know from the beginning that their love affair is doomed, but are powerless to alter their fate. Deirdre, before she was ever born, was foretold by the Druids to be the ruination of Ulster and, later known as Deirdre of the Sorrows, threw herself to her death from her chariot. As the Celts suffered successive invasions and conquests, their legends reflected the precariousness of the warrior's life, nostalgia for past greatness, and a recognition that adversity must be patiently endured.

THE STORY OF OISIN AND NIAV

The love-story of Oisin and Niav also ends sadly, but with a twist of humour from the monk who recorded it. Finn MacCool, leader of the Fianna, the warriors who guarded the High King of Ireland, was hunting with his son Oisin by Loch Lene when they saw a lovely girl on a white horse, riding across the waters towards them. She was Niav of the Golden Hair, daughter of the King of Tir Nan Og, the Land of Eternal Youth. She was in love with Oisin and had come to seek his hand in marriage. Oisin fell in love with Niav at once, climbed up behind her, and they galloped off together.

They crossed the ocean and arrived at the Land of Eternal Youth where Oisin was instantly changed into the Ever-Young. He and Niav were married

LEFT: Deirdre cradles the severed head of her murdered lover.

and her father left for the Land of Silence. They ruled in his place for timeless centuries, deeply in love, until Oisin began to pine for Ireland, his father, Finn, and his own folk.

Niav lent him her white horse but warned him that his feet must never touch the ground. Oisin rode over the ocean to Ireland, but it was changed and the ancient home of the Fianna was overgrown with grass. Riding back to the sea, he fell from his horse and immediately became the oldest man in the world. But St Patrick was passing by and baptized him, so Oisin died a good Christian and went to heaven.

ABOVE: Oisin and Niav journey towards the Land of Eternal Youth.

RIGHT: Years later on his return, Oisin falls from his horse and instantly loses his magical youth.

THE SOURCE OF INSPIRATION

Wisdom, inspiration and the gift of prophecy could be bestowed by inhabitants of the Otherworld, often in miraculous cauldrons containing magical potions.

THE GREAT CAULDRON

Various magical cauldrons crop up again and again in Celtic mythology. Sometimes it was a vessel which fed everyone, at other times it was a huge pot that brought dead warriors back to life. Sometimes the cauldron may have had a part to play in sacrifice and always it was something to be sought through hardship and great peril, possessed and fought over. In Christian times it became the Holy Grail, identified with the Chalice of Jesus's Last Supper.

LEFT: The Gundestrup cauldron. 1st century AD.

GUARDIANS OF THE CAULDRON

The Dagda, the "Good God", is guardian of the Cauldron. Bran, a later god-like chieftain, also has a cauldron. Its properties include an ability to satisfy the hunger and thirst of all and sundry, and to bring the dead back to life. The great poet and prophet, Taliesin, came to his bardic illumination after sipping inspiration – the Celts called it Awen – from the forbidden cauldron of the goddess Ceridwen. Another seer was Myrddin (who appears in the Arthurian stories as Merlin), probably a historical figure of the early Christian period. Having lost his wits following a great battle, his return to sanity seems to owe much to a fairy woman or priestess of Ceridwen.

The cauldron has a significance beyond the Celtic world. The Germanic goddess Nerthus supervised the ritual drowning of her victims and, embossed on the great Gundestrup Cauldron there is a goddess plunging soldiers into it. Is this an act of sacrifice, or is it for bringing them back to life? We don't know for certain.

BELOW: A detail from the Gundestrup cauldron.

WISDOM, MANIPULATION AND POWER

Annwn, the Otherworld, was the source of inspiration. It also offered the temptations of manipulation and power. From Annwn, the poets sought Awen, their bardic inspiration, and from Annwn the druids also sought the authority which enabled them to impose *geas* (prohibitions) upon chiefs and kings. Each *geas* carried with it an implied curse: "If you do this, something terrible will happen!" It was a taboo that could apply to the speaking of names, the eating of certain foods, or the participation in a forbidden activity. It was used by the druids as protection – the *geas* represented influence through fear.

Idris was a Welsh giant. With Gwydion, son of Don, and Gwynn, son of Nudd, he was one of the three great astronomers of Britain. He was said to map the heavens and knew the future, until the day of doom. The summit of Cader Idris, or "Idris' Chair", was a dreadful place, for if a man spent the night there he must surely be found, when morning came, either dead, mad, or filled with Awen. This mythology indicates both the temptations and the perils of seeking to penetrate the mysteries of the Otherworld. It also suggests its rewards but includes the warning that death, or madness, lies in wait for the presumptuous.

RIGHT: Another of the goddesses associated with the legends of Arthur, the Damsel of the Holy Grail.

MYSTICISM AND THE LAND

In Celtic culture, the spiritual and material worlds were interconnected and humanity was part of nature, each being enriched by the other. Poetic inspiration came directly from natural forces.

ABOVE: Rolling Irish hills interact with the flat sea.

An example of this is the Celtic idea of kingship, which depended upon a relationship with the Mother Goddess, a force of nature. This relationship meant that the land did not belong to the people but that the people belonged to the land. There was a sacral, even a nuptial relationship between king and Goddess.

The Celts inherited the traditions and religious practices of older peoples and one of the ways of seeking Awen, or poetic inspiration, was by lying in the dark in a cave or rock chamber, usually at a site regarded as specially potent for the purpose, and awaiting visions and inspirations. It may be that this formed part of an initiatory process.

The bards and the druids, together with other individuals, put great emphasis on Awen, inspiration and insights from Annwn, the Otherworld, or what might now be described in Jungian terms as the collective unconscious. In the same way the later, Celtic-Christian, mystics sought an eternally loving union with God in mystical prayer. There was no such notion of love between the pagan gods and humanity, however, who were essentially natural forces and archetypes to be known through mythology and to be propitiated out of fear.

BELOW: Land and water are joined but distinct.

The song of a water sprite, the song of a bird, or the improvisations of a Celtic fiddle player were all regarded as one. Folk music is directly derived from and inspired by nature. Both the song of a bird and the improvisations of a musician are spontaneous and unconscious. Celtic people communicated with each other and their environment through music and dance, as do their descendants today.

BELOW: An Irish-Celtic standing stone from around the 1st century bears continual witness to human endeavour.

ABOVE: Nature and humanity are as one in the landscape.

THE EXPRESSION OF NATURE

The strong sense of identification of Celtic people with the land remains to the present day. It finds expression in music and dance. Dance expresses both earthly and cosmic relationships, and also the mysteries of love and of war. Folk music is an expression of the folk singer's or musician's affiliation with nature and the landscape.

LOOKING FOR INNER SILENCE

Celtic mysticism is a timeless appreciation of a reality beyond the everyday, which is just as relevant today as in the bygone age of Celtic paganism. Its basis is an awareness of harmony with nature and the unity of Creation.

Mysticism, in any shape or form, depends upon inner silence and self-awareness. This involves removing external noises and distractions and then trying to remove all the internal noise which modern life stirs up within you. A well-tried Celtic tradition, used by poets until quite recent times, involves lying down in a quiet, darkened room, with a flat stone on the stomach. Choose a time when you know you will not be disturbed so that you feel free to let your mind drift completely. The stone should be just heavy enough to prevent sleep and just light enough not to be positively uncomfortable. With a blindfold over the eyes and silence without, you can begin the task of seeking silence within.

Let a poem arise out of your depths. Don't try too hard. Try not to think. Be as silent as you can and allow words to come to the surface. Keep silent for as long as you can. When the time seems right, come back to the world and write down what came to you. Never mind if it seems half-finished or makes little sense. It is the inner silence that matters and this is an ancient Celtic way of seeking it.

ABOVE: Shut out the common light of day.
RIGHT: In a quiet place seek the silence within.

ABOVE: Return to the light of day illuminated from within.

Experience the touch and texture of a stone.

Listen to the wind in the trees and feel the sun.

Look closely and enter into the wonder of plant life.

Discover the beauty of nature's tiny things.

INSPIRATION FROM NATURE

The threads of creation weave together to form a tapestry of great beauty. The art and culture of the Celts reflects their vision of interconnectedness and their drawing of inspiration from the world of nature is something all too often forgotten in modern Western society.

Simply going for a walk can bring you closer to the earth and more in tune with its natural cycles. Meditating under a tree or in a cave can heighten awareness of the totality of which we are a part.

Find a place that is special to you, where you feel a sense

RIGHT: Nature is a trans-figured image of its creator.

of belonging. Be still there and notice what is all about you: trees, grass, water, sky, animals and insects.

Close your eyes and breathe deeply to relax yourself. With your eyes closed you can expand your other senses. Hear the wind in the trees, water lapping, insects moving. Smell the scents carried on the breeze and rising up from all around. Chew a blade of grass and discover its sweetness. Feel the texture of a stone.

Try to extend your senses further. Feel what is beneath the soil, in the sky: roots burrowing, clouds scudding, the very earth breathing.

When you open your eyes appreciate the experience of being for what it is, both humbling and inspiring.

A Journey to Annwn

The Celt looks naturally towards the setting sun. The Gaelic Tir Nan Og is an island in the west. The British Avalon – Island of Apples – belongs to Annwn, the Otherworld. There, Arthur lies, listening to fairy music. Some speculate that Avalon, the grave of Arthur, is that invisible island in Llyn Tegid, where Ceridwen's cauldron was once said to be. There are other contenders for this lost land, but a Celtic tradition continues of a white barge that takes the soul to its home in the Land of Eternal Youth.

THE OTHERWORLD

Celtic art and culture reflect the inspiration drawn from nature but inspiration was also sought from Annwn, the place from which they sprang and to which they would return. The Celts, with their sense of universal interconnectedness, saw the Otherworld as an extension of this world which could be reached by various "gateways".

To undertake a shamanic journey in the creative imagination requires little other than an objective to seek and a desire to seek it. You will need to find a place where you won't be disturbed. Spend a while becoming fully recollected and focussing on why you are making this journey and what you hope to find when you reach the Otherworld in your imagination. When you are fully "centred" in yourself, lie down and close your eyes.

You are looking for an entrance into the earth. It might be a cave or a cleft in the rock, a well or a spring, but you will know the entrance to Annwn when you see it.

RIGHT: The living flame, symbol of light within.

RIGHT: Release your mind and let your creative imagination take you on a journey.

ABOVE: Return deliberately and extinguish the flame of your candle.

Enter without fear, but with respect. This is a magical realm where anything is possible. You may meet obstacles, animals or people that bar your way. Use your creative imagination to get round them.

You may meet helpers, who could take any form: people you have known, others you do not recognize, spirits or even gods and goddesses. You can also change your own shape or appearance. Be determined in your aim and resourceful in the way that you confront difficulties, don't be frightened or turned aside by anything in your way.

When you return at the end of your journey, focus yourself firmly back into normal consciousness. Go over the journey and write it down. Your concentration will improve the more you practise.

RIGHT: Use the images and tales of the ancient world as inspiration.

MEETING THE ARCHETYPES

The Celtic myths and legends are a tangled web of stories, handed down over untold generations by poets and storytellers, and only recorded in writing less than fifteen hundred years ago. The myths and their characters are archetypal; they originate from our deepest tribal and collective memories. Essentially, they are about humanity. To read the stories and to meet the characters is to meet parts of our own selves, including parts that we may not like very much. Read them and get to know them. They are the foundation upon which great things were built.

ABOVE: Druid priestess with sacred mistletoe.

Archetypes are aspects of ourselves that may hold the answers to what we are seeking. Meeting with an archetype in meditation is a way of gaining access to the unconscious. By giving the unconscious a form, using the creative imagination, it is easier to access and communicate with it. By calling upon a bard or a druid, a hero or a heroine, insights and strengths can be called up from within ourselves.

A FORM FOR A MEDITATION

First of all tell yourself, aloud, what you want to do and who you want to meet. Then find somewhere where you will not be disturbed, settle yourself comfortably and breathe deeply to become relaxed.

Visualize yourself in the hall of a Celtic chief. A fire burns in the central hearth and its flickering light illuminates the roof timbers and the thatch. You are seated in a carved chair on a low dais, ready

LEFT: A druid, a potential source of wisdom, knowledge and inspiration.
RIGHT: Morgan le Fay, crafty witch and seductress.

ABOVE: Cuchulainn, the archetypal warrior.

ABOVE: Tell yourself clearly what your intentions are.

RIGHT: Relax, visualize, concentrate on the detail.

ABOVE: While the images are clear in your mind, write down what you have learned and return to it in a few days to seek further illumination.

to receive whoever shall come to you. (In other words, you are in control.) When you feel truly there, call on the archetype you want to talk to.

Be courteous when you meet and ask the name of whoever you have called. Tell whoever it is why he or she has been called and what you want of them. Don't forget to thank your archetype when the meeting is concluded.

Return, quite deliberately, to full and normal consciousness (this is important, take some time to ensure that you have achieved this) and write down what you have learned.

Concentration during this kind of meditation can be hard to maintain at first, but it comes with practice. You may find the same archetypes keep returning or you may encounter new ones each time. They may tell you about themselves, and therefore something about yourself at the same time. Treat them with respect as they can be quite formidable, even a bit disturbing. They are connected with human nature, and are therefore quite uninhibited. Meditate on them, talk to them in your imagination, but do not try to force answers from them during your dialogues. They will teach you more than you expect.

CHAPTER TWO

THE FULFILMENT OF CELTIC PAGANISM

When the Celts became Christian, the ancient myths were said to have been fulfilled in history. Heaven had "married" Earth and Mary, a real woman of flesh and blood, had fulfilled all the mythology of the goddess. She had "named and armed" her Son, who was the real, historical redemptive sacrifice, validated by his witnessed resurrection from the dead. And the Christian's Good God was experienced by them as a Trinity, like the triple aspects of the ancient Celtic deities. It was a natural progression from the best in paganism, and it was about love, not fear.

THE PAGAN CELTS

*Pagan religion has its dark side. There is evidence of human sacrifice, although Roman
accounts of this may be more propagandist than reliable. It is a great mistake, however,
to regard pagan religion and religious practice as necessarily dark and fear-ridden.
Much of it was assimilated, without difficulty, into a later Christianity
that was perceived as fulfilling it.*

To see how Christianity was seen and recognized by the Celts as a belief system they could assimilate it is necessary first to explore the pagan beliefs the Celts held in the pre-Christian era. The Great Mother is mother both of the gods and of the Celtic people and the Great Mother is, of course, the Earth Mother herself. As is typical of Celtic deities, she has three names: Anu, Danu and Don. The hills in Kerry, "the Paps of Anu", reflect one aspect, while as Danu she is mother of the Irish gods and as Don she is the

BELOW: An artist's impression of a pagan Celtic burial.

ancestor of the British gods. As the Earth Mother is reflected in the landscape, so all sovereignty depends upon the people's relationship with her. The poets adapted the tribal myths to conform to their local landscape in order to establish a sense of authority which was part of the Celtic people's security.

THE GOOD GOD
The name Dagda means the "Good God". His two other names, Eochaid Ollathair, "Father of All", and Ruadh Rofessa, "Red One of Perfect Knowledge", describe the one who performed miracles and saw to the weather and the harvest. The male deity is a more shadowy figure than the Goddess and there is a confused, and confusing, mythology about him. He is styled King of the Tuatha de Danaan, the pre-Gaelic Irish who now dwell under the Earth.

THE MORRIGHAN AND BRIGIT
The Morrighan is a formidable female personality, a persona of the Goddess who was the king's champion and protector of the land. The threefold Morrigna – Morrighan and her sisters – appeared at the death of a king or hero, often in the guise of

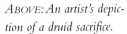

ABOVE: An artist's depiction of a druid sacrifice.

RIGHT: Standing stones represent an ancient link between man and gods.

carrion crows. At Cuchulainn's death, the Morrighan perched on his shoulder as a black crow. The trio of Arthur's half-sisters, including Morgan le Fay, echoed this complex legendary figure.

A more comfortable personality is Brigit, daughter of Dagda and patron of poets, smiths and healers. She was the Fair Maid of Spring and, in the Outer Hebrides, rites of Brigit were known almost within living memory. An image of Brigit as a young maid was dressed in white, a crystal was placed over its heart and it was invited into the house to the singing of songs and ancient chants. These were women's rites, performed at the turn of the Celtic year, and had primarily to do with new birth.

THE CULT OF THE HEAD

The human head was a symbol for the Celts of divine power and, as the seat of the soul, a link with the ancestral spirits. During times of war the severed heads of enemies were collected and fixed to the doorposts of forts and houses. It was thought that the heads protected the buildings, a belief that persisted well into the medieval period.

The head of the legendary British king, Bran the Blessed, was cut off by his own troops after his defeat in Ireland, and continued to eat and speak during the voyage home. By tradition it was buried in London and still lies under the Tower of London, protecting Britain from invasion.

RESPECT FOR THE OLD WAYS

A respect for all that had gone before characterized the relatively speedy conversion of the Celtic people to the Christian faith. Our knowledge of this conversion is centred, in the main, on a large number of outstanding individuals who succeeded, not in arbitrarily abolishing the past and attempting to start again from scratch, but rather in "baptizing" what had gone before.

FULFILMENT, NOT CONDEMNATION

"The sober Christianity of Patrick and the wild paganism of the Celts" were, according to one Irish writer, the dual influences on his boyhood. What had gone before was not denied or condemned, it was

BELOW: Launcelot fights the dragon.

ABOVE: Launcelot by the deathbed of Guinevere.

baptized and fulfilled. If a party of Celtic warriors had turned up for Mass on a Sunday morning, "my eyes would have been surprised, but not my imagination or my faith," he wrote. It was in fact the Celtic Christian monks of the fifth century who had recorded the legends for posterity, because they represented the nature that divine grace would glorify.

Arthur straddles the Celtic and Christian traditions with each claiming him as their own. Arthur was a king caught between the old order and the new. His queen, Guinevere, comes from Annwn, as her name, beginning with "Gwyn" (white), reveals. Her lover, Launcelot (of the Lake – Annwn), is related, mythologically, to the Celtic sun hero. The whole Arthuriad is Celtic mythology, baptized and – in the Grail legends – transformed into a Christian layman's spirituality. Nothing of value is lost.

ABOVE: The Irish saint, Patrick, a Celtic Christian.

Ireland was evangelized. Patrick and his companions knew how to present the Christian faith to them, without compromise but with respect for them and for the best of their old ways.

CONVERSION BY CHARACTER

What converted Ireland, however, was not Patrick's eloquence but his holiness. He seemed quite different from other men; he knew God as his friend. Patrick is associated with many wild and lonely places in Ireland; places which he loved. Alone with the wild beauty of land, sea and sky all about him, he could lose himself in the Love of God and take it all with him in his heart. This is what the essence of Celtic mysticism is all about.

BELOW: St Colmcille (Columba) blesses his old horse.

COMMUNICATING WITH RESPECT

St Paul preached the Christian gospel in Athens, using a pagan altar inscription as his starting-point. St Patrick did very much the same in Ireland. Patrick had been captured by Irish pirates in his youth and was a slave until he escaped. He returned to Ireland as a bishop. He understood the Irish and their beliefs and, within the space of a lifetime,

THE BAPTISM OF A PAGAN GODDESS

The pagan concepts of deity were not so much denied as corrected. In some cases they were even "baptized". Brigit, as Fair Maid of Spring, was a pagan goddess who inspired affection. Hers was a positive dynamic and she has been assimilated into a historical figure who was probably named after her. Brigit, or Bride, a contemporary of St Patrick, was the daughter of a wealthy pagan, Dubthach, and his bondswoman, Broicsech. Bride became a Christian and dedicated herself to Christ as a nun. Bishop Mel, who received her vocation, is said to have consecrated her as a bishop, claiming divine command, despite the objections of others present. St Bride of Kildare was a Christlike woman, much loved in her lifetime.

THE EARTH MOTHER OF GOD

Bride, now a composite figure of Christian saint and pagan goddess, is popularly associated with the Virgin Mary. Her feast day is the Celtic spring festival of Imbolc at the beginning of February, which is also Candlemas, the feast of the Purification of the Blessed Virgin Mary. Celtic Christian mythology has her searching with Mary for the missing boy Jesus in the temple, and she is also said to have been Mary's midwife at the birth of Jesus in the stable at Bethlehem. Such is Bride's association with the Mother of God that she is sometimes called "Mary of the Gaels". The Blessed Virgin herself fulfils all the essential, and necessary, functions of the Earth Mother.

LEFT: The head of a Celtic goddess.

ABOVE: A Holy Well, probably once a Celtic shrine to a pagan god.

THE ONCE-PAGAN MIDWIFE OF CHRIST

Bride, baptized by identification with St Bride, may not have been Mary's midwife historically, but in the profoundest sense she was Mary's midwife mythologically. Christians understand the Incarnation as the fulfilment, not only of the Old Testament

ABOVE: *Celtic goddess, child and bird, from the Gundestrup Cauldron.*

RIGHT: *A burial chamber, symbolic of a doorway from this world to another.*

hope, but also of the very best of paganism. The Celts embraced the Christian faith so quickly because it fulfilled them. It did not deny their past but rather baptized it and gave them a new and eternal hope and a personal relationship with God. They continued to revere the natural world but now, instead of existing in its own right, it was seen as the handiwork of God. In this sense, though the Hebrew Mary was acknowledged as the Mother of God, the Celtic Bride was a faithful midwife indeed.

A NATURAL PROGRESSION

Christian men and women, whose work and witness were seen to be Christ-like, and who had served and often healed their fellow men and women, gradually took the places of the ancient gods in the popular imagination. Wells and other ancient holy places began to be dedicated, no longer to nature spirits, but rather to the local Saint who had often used their waters for baptism and for healing. They remained holy places, dedicated to a personality, not of fear but of love.

The Celtic Sun God Walks the Earth

The Celts, like many pagan and classical religions, included in their pantheon a Sun God whose coming to earth would herald an age of prosperity, health and happiness. Many new converts saw Jesus as fulfilment of this myth, and the dawn of a new order.

Respect for other people and their beliefs is an obligation of love. The Irish Church was organized around tribal monasteries and Colmcille or Columba (AD521–97), a prince of the northern Ui Neill, became a monk and a great founder of monastic communities in Ireland. He was a noted scholar and scribe who produced a famous copy of the Psalms. However, his family became embroiled in a dispute with the High King Diarmid – of the rival, southern Ui Neill – which ended in the battle of Cul Dreibne, on the slopes of Ben Bulben. Colmcille was implicated and, tormented in conscience, exiled himself to Scotland, sailing with 12 companions across the Irish Sea to the deserted island of Iona, which he made his base. From there he ministered to the Irish enclave of Dal Riada in Argyll and set about preaching the Christian faith in Scotland and the north of England.

On Iona, the formerly hawk-like Colmcille began to live up to his name, which means "dove of the Church". One story tells how, arriving in a pagan community, he said to the chief druid: "Your religion looks forward to a time when the Sun God walks the Earth and all shall be healed. I have good news! He has come, and his name is Jesus."

RIGHT: St Colmcille or Columba of Iona.

SAINT COLUMBA

ABOVE: Columba's cell and St Martin's cross, Iona.

REASON AND INSPIRATION

Awen, inspiration, is bound up with the human faculty of intuition or the inner "way of knowing". The intuition has to be challenged by reason or a man or woman can become unbalanced in one direction. But reason has also to be informed – and sometimes questioned – by the intuition, or the individual becomes equally unbalanced in the opposite direction; an all too common fault in modern, western society. The Celtic saints reveal a refreshing, and altogether too rare, wholeness.

Colmcille, better known by his Latinized name Columba, was a very talented and accomplished human being. He was a great scholar with a powerful, reasoning mind. But, being a Celt, he was also highly intuitive. He could "see through" people and situations, and he was thought by his followers to possess an uncanny ability to foresee the future. This story of his life shows the otherworldly air that he was thought to have when on one occasion he postponed a fast because he felt someone was about to visit the monastery and it would have been unkind to expect him to fast. The next day, sure enough, the completely unexpected visitor arrived.

BELOW: Iona Abbey.

LOVE AND RESPECT FOR ALL CREATION

*The transition from paganism to Christianity did not diminish the Celtic
sense of spirituality permeating the natural world.*

A story which typifies the Celt's respect for animal creation is that of Melangell. She may have been Irish or may have been the daughter of a Cumbrian chief. She ran away from her family to escape a forced marriage to another chief. She came to a beautiful little *nant*, or blind valley, in the mountains of Powys, built a hut and lived the life of a Christian hermit. One day Brochwel Ysgithrog, Prince of Powys, was hunting hares. A terrified hare ran from the hounds and hid under Melangell's skirt. The dogs backed off and the huntsman could not command them. Up rode the prince.

"I found sanctuary in this valley and the hare has found sanctuary with me!" said Melangell to Brochwel. He asked for her story and, much moved by her courage and compassion for small creatures, he called off his hounds and graciously gave the *nant* to her as her hermitage. She is buried in the little shrine church at Pennant Melangell and her saintly presence still permeates the whole place. It

ABOVE: St Melangell's shrine, Powys.

LEFT: St Melangell's Shrine Church, Pennant Melangell, Powys.

ABOVE: Early Celtic Christian saints were often famed for their care and understanding of the animal kingdom.

is not surprising to learn that more than one visitor to this remote church has been greeted by a large hare who has led them to the church door before bounding off out of sight.

RESPECT FOR THE LITTLE THINGS

One of the most attractive personalities of the early Celtic church is Dewi Sant (St David). He founded his monastery at the place which now bears his name when that corner of Wales was under Irish occupation. Dewi's community became a haven of Welsh language and culture, both of which were then under threat. It was said that he spent all of every day, "inflexibly and unweariedly teaching, praying, caring for the brethren and feeding orphans, widows, the needy, the sick, the feeble and pilgrims." He was a tireless founder of Christian communities and, according to legend, provided a hive of bees for each one of them.

One witness said of Dewi that, "He took bread and cress, or water from cold rivers; and wore a full-length horse-hair garment, and did penance beside a spring." Dewi's final message to his followers was: "Brothers and sisters, be happy and keep your faith and your belief, and do the little things that you have heard and seen me do." The little things are the things that really matter, that among other things express respect for all that has gone before.

RIGHT: A traditional dome-shaped bee hive.

PRAYERS AND OFFERINGS

Prayer, in all its forms, is essentially an expression of a relationship.
It is something which is done, not just something which is said.

Much of pagan prayer was too often an expression of fearful relationships and was propitiatory in character. True prayer, in its widest sense, embraces all manner of relationships; between ourselves and God, between ourselves and the saints, the angels and the faithful departed and between ourselves and the rest of creation. Like the ancient Celtic myths, Gaelic prayers and incantations were transmitted orally, so

BELOW: Votive offerings. Medron Holy Well, Cornwall.

that their immediacy and relevance was passed on.

Around the holy wells and holy places in Ireland remarkable collections of small objects may be found, left there by individuals who have prayed there. The leaving of a token "a little something" is an instinctive courtesy, a symbol that the relationship has been expressed. It is a very human gesture and it is found in many different traditions around the world. In Christian churches it is found in the lighting of votive candles, in folk traditions it can be seen in various local customs, but it can also be a personal ritual that is devised and carried out by an individual. Leaving an offering is a satisfying gesture to make, expressive of both respect and affection. It is also an important part of human life, a recognition of the ebb and flow of energy in the relationship between the human world and heaven. It shows that an exchange has taken place, and is also an expression of gratitude. It matters little what the token is, as long as it is something that has meaning for you.

ABOVE: Holy Well, Alsia, Cornwall.

MAKING AN OFFERING OUTSIDE

If you pray indoors, you might like to set aside a particular place as a permanent shrine and leave your offering there. If you pray out of doors leave the token at the base of a tree, or on a rock. Christian believers might use an icon or a cross as their focal point for prayer; but all will have their own personal ways of focussing. Prayer, rightly understood, is a universal activity.

Find a place where you can feel a spiritual connection. Hold the chosen token in your left palm, offer it up to the sky and down to the Earth, and to the four Airts – the four quarters or cardinal points – and allow your heart to feel thankful.

Speak your gratitude aloud, to reinforce your intent, then place the offering on your temporary shrine or in the place you have chosen.

ABOVE: It matters little what the offering is as long as it has meaning for you. Salt is a long-used token.

To complete the ritual, close it in the traditional way by drawing a circle in the air above the offering with your hand and then quartering the circle with a cross.

Offer the token to the Sky, to the Earth and to the Four Airts.

With care and reverence, place the token in the place you have chosen.

With two fingers, sign the circle and the cross to complete the ritual.

CHAPTER THREE

MYSTICISM: AN ATTITUDE OF MIND AND HEART

The central part of Celtic mysticism, both before and after the
Christian period, is that faith and life are regarded as one.
Daily prayer would begin with an extension of the Gaelic
tradition of ortha *— incantations that consecrated the daily*
household chores. The light of the new day was seen as a foretaste
of "the guiding light of eternity". This is a profoundly mystical
approach to life; it is an attitude of mind that is firmly
integrated with the heart.

CREATION IN THE IMAGE OF ITS CREATOR

*For Celtic Christians, the perfection of the natural world they saw around them
was the ultimate manifestation of God's supreme creative power.*

A Welsh poet wrote of the sweetness of nature, buried in black winter's grave, and then, in spring, spoke of the willow, whose harp had hung silent, giving forth its melody. "Listen!" he cried, "The

world is alive!" An Irish bard sang of a storm at sea, of the ocean's wild, troubled sleep, and of the hair of the wife of Manannan (the sea god), being tossed about. Another poem has news for us of the coming of winter: the stag is calling, cold has seized the bird's wing. The whole of nature is alive, it is all of an unutterable beauty and it is nothing less than the glorified image of its creator.

The Celtic poets of the Dark Ages and the early medieval period wrote of nature with both love and a deep awe. An Irish hermit described his hut in the woods, known only to himself and God. He wrote of the heather, the honeysuckle, the stags, the birds, "the grave and peaceful host of the country-side" all about his door, all for him to love, and in all of whom he found God, "All the gift of my dear Christ."

THE CELTIC VISION OF NATURE

The Celtic vision derives from a paganism which found its fulfilment by assimilation into the Christian faith. There remains an awareness that the Celts belong to the land, the land does not belong to them. The land is associated with the Goddess, the Earth Mother, however remote this may be from

LEFT: A stag in autumn heralding the change of season.

ABOVE: Spring blossom.

intuitive awareness and the fullest exercise of reason. Where reason is exalted at the complete expense of the intuitive faculty, there is no possibility of mysticism, and neither is any true mysticism possible where reason is abandoned. A true mysticism demands equilibrium, a balance of the faculties and an openness to the realities of things. Mysticism must always keep its feet on the ground.

BELOW: Snowdrops in the snow.

conscious awareness. Mary, the Mother of God, and her mythical companion, Bride, maintain this connection. A "marriage" of Heaven and Earth brought forth the Incarnation and thus both the biblical and the pagan hopes were fulfilled.

Mysticism depends on the mind being receptive to such a connection. Such a mind is open to both

RELIGION INTERWOVEN WITH LIFE

There is no separation of religion from life in Celtic spirituality. God is in all things and all things are in God; the Earth is a living organism. Heaven is invisible but is all about us and everything that exists is a potential source of blessing. It is as natural to wish for the Heavenly Host to be seated at one's own table as it was natural for publicans and sinners to invite Christ himself to eat with them, and in both cases the invitation was accepted through love.

A CEILIDH FOR THE KING OF HEAVEN

An Irish poet, seeing himself as a tenant of his Lord, the King of Heaven, sought to pay his legal dues of lodging and hospitality. He wrote of his longing to give a great ale-feast for the King of Heaven, and for all the Heavenly Host to be seated at his table forever, feasting and drinking to their hearts' content. He wanted Jesus Christ never to leave the feast, and for the "Three Marys" to grace it with their presence also. He wanted forever to be rent-payer to the Lord and to be able to pay his dues with all the hospitality of his heart.

BELOW: Jesus feasting at the wedding at Cana, the Celtic ideal of a lord feasting with his followers.

ABOVE: A monolith in Co Kerry, Ireland.

THE VISION OF WHOLENESS

There is nothing slight or sentimental about Celtic spirituality, it is grounded in a deep realism. It is quite wrong to romanticize it or to imagine that all things were at all times nothing but sweetness and light. Nor are all Celts themselves necessarily natural mystics; true mystics are rare in any generation. What is distinctive about Celtic

RIGHT: Irish gold torque, c. 1st century BC.

spirituality, as it has evolved through the centuries from paganism to a mature Christian faith, is its realism. It is close to nature and open both to intuition and to reason. There is a sense of unity between all the elements of life: the angels, the saints, the farmer and his cow.

The Celtic world was shielded by force of historical circumstances from influences which over the years tended to obscure the Church's vision of this holistic approach. There is, for example, nothing of the disturbed and disturbing equation

BELOW: A romantic nineteenth-century impression of druid women dancing round the menhir.

ABOVE: Earth and the wonder of the heavens.

of sex with sin, or any implication that material creation is in some way imperfect, which have hung about the edges of the Church's mind, though wholly foreign to the teaching of the gospels. Celtic spirituality is essentially primitive and rooted in a oneness with nature.

ḥEAVEN INTERWOVEN WITH ƐARTH

Heaven permeates earth and earthly life in the Celtic vision. The whole of life – as recorded in hymns, incantations, prayers and even magic spells – is a continuous experience of the frontier between heaven and earth. This is a frontier of consciousness, not a physical line drawn on the ground. The character of heaven is not that of Annwn, one of darkness tinged with fear, it is one of light, life and above all, love.

INTERWOVEN REALITIES

Heaven, though unseen, is all about us. Day-to-day life is lived in the context of a heaven which is only just out of normal human sight. The fisherman asks that the king of the elements, Christ himself, be seated at the helm. The mystery of seed-sowing is celebrated with its own *ortha*, or incantation. The sower will go round his field sun-wise, with the angels and the apostles for company and in the full sight of the Blessed Trinity. He will begin his harvest on the feast of the Archangel Michael and raise the first cut of the sickle, turning it three times round his head in honour of the Trinity.

HEAVEN AT HOME

Mary and Bride encircle the hearth, the floor and the entire household. The holy apostles are present, unseen. By the bed is Bride and her fosterling, the Christ-Child. The Mother of God watches over the household and Christ himself, the king of the sun, is always at your shoulder. A morning song must be sung to God, for Mary's lark is singing it in the

LEFT: The Archangel Michael defeats Satan.

clouds and every other living creature is singing its song of love. Will you alone be dumb?

The Mother of God, the holy Archangel Michael and "gentle Bride of the locks of gold" are invoked to "keep my feet on the just path." Heaven is completely interwoven with earth. The darkness of Annwn is lit up by the light of heaven.

THE ANGELS AND THE COW

A *sain* (blessing) is placed upon sheep, with the sign of the cross, as protection against all that may harm them. Cattle are entrusted to the care of St Columba, St Brigit (Bride) and Mary the Mother of God. When the cattle come home

ABOVE: Another battle between good and evil as Michael casts down the devil.

they are met with a song of welcome, *failte a' chruidh*, to which they respond, sometimes lowing, sometimes bellowing. This is to acknowledge that the Three Persons of the Blessed Trinity have kept the precious cattle from harm and brought them safely home. And at the milking, the aid of the angels and the saints is asked to persuade the young cow to take to her calf.

The *ortha* are of great antiquity. The incantations or chantings assimilated the pieties of pagan Celts and transformed them. They were passed down orally from generation to generation and were only collected and recorded in the 19th century. They represent a genuine mysticism of the hearth, a religious sense of ceremony that is woven into every day life.

PEARLS AND SWINE

It has been said that "the mind is the slayer of the real." Our faculty of reason is quick to rationalize and to try to "explain away" anything that is out of the ordinary. A deep, inner experience, be it psychical in nature or mystical, is quickly "psychologized", and thus denied, by many other people who do not share the same awareness. Jesus referred to this when he warned his listeners not to "cast pearls before swine." The pearls are the inner realities, the inner experiences and awarenesses that we are given, which are self-authenticating by virtue of their essential character.

MAKING PILGRIMAGES

The word pilgrimage suggests the making of a considerable physical effort. Present-day pilgrimages often involve long walks over many days. This is a valuable exercise for all concerned, for the journey (an touras) is inward as much as it is outward. Once this fact is grasped, then it is possible to make pilgrimages involving considerable inward journeys but quite small outward manifestations of them. Pilgrimage, like mysticism, is first of all the attitude of a mind firmly fixed within the heart. A periodic journey to the heart, perhaps a daily journey, is a good way of acquiring a mystical habit of mind.

LOOK FOR THE SMALLEST THINGS

Eternity, said the poet, is in a grain of sand. Make a point of looking for the smallest things: the tiniest flower, the minute details of lichen, the patterns created in nature, especially the smallest ones. Look at minute creatures with a new eye and learn to wonder at them. Look at your own hand and try to realize that if you were looking at it through a microscope powerful enough, it would look like a universe of infinitesimal stars with unimaginable spaces between them. We are made of energy, held together by an intention. Make small regular

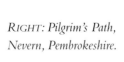

LEFT: *A fifteenth-century manuscript showing the progression of a pilgrimage in France.*

RIGHT: *Pilgrim's Path, Nevern, Pembrokeshire.*

RIGHT: A depiction of the goddess of day and night.

pilgrimages in search of tiny things. Remember Dewi Sant's (St David's) advice: "Do the little things." On a starry night, try to escape the light-pollution and the noise-pollution of the town and sit silently, listening to the stars. Think it possible and you will succeed. Remember that the ancient Celts perceived the stars as living creatures.

TO MAKE A PILGRIMAGE

Sit silently with your spine straight and your head erect. Concentrate your imagination on drawing your mind down into your heart on an inward journey.

If necessary, whisper a short word such as "love" to keep distracting thoughts from flooding in. This will act like cats' eyes in the road when driving on a foggy night.

LEFT: Look out for and honour the little things.

A single word, uttered every so often, will keep you out of the ditch of distractions.

Imagine holding your mind in your heart's silence for as long as you can, and then come quietly back to normal consciousness.

Don't try to intellectualize things, just learn to let them be what they are. This is an important part of learning the lifetime's task of letting yourself be what you really are and not what you think you are.

BELOW: Imagine an inward journey into your heart.

TRUE MYSTICISM

The words "mysticism" and "mystical" are often used to describe what might better be referred to as "the supernatural". It is all too easy to confuse the two. A mystic is not one who encounters ghosts or the fairies, nor is mysticism concerned with Annwn, the Otherworld. A true mystic is one who responds to the direct and intuitive knowledge of God, or Ultimate Reality, that is attained through personal experience.

NATURE AND GRACE

Christians from the earliest times have used the word grace to describe the transforming power of God the Holy Spirit within a human soul. The work of grace is to take what is already present in the human spirit, that of nature, and bring it to fulfilment on a wholly other level of being.

Grace re-creates from within; needless to say it does so only with the soul's fullest co-operation and it is at the very least a lifetime's work. Psychism is a natural gift in everyone, though it remains dormant in many. It belongs to nature. The work of grace is to transform psychism to another level altogether,

BELOW: The meeting of this world and the world of the fairies is often a theme in the Arthurian legends.

from Annwn to heaven, or mysticism. Fairies may be good but angels are better.

Mysticism belongs, we might say, to the "grace level" of things and not to the "nature level". Bringing the mind into the heart is a work of the human will, aided by grace. It is grace which opens our eyes and enables us to see things in a new way. It allows us to forget ourselves in contemplation of the wonder and beauty of nature all about us through which we gain an insight into the true nature of life. True mysticism is a gift of grace, working with our own little efforts and best intentions.

CELTIC REALISM

Dewi Sant (St David) realized the need for attention to detail when he said "Do the little things." If the little things are done the big things take care of themselves. This is Jesus' teaching in the gospels and it illustrates the realism which characterizes Celtic spirituality. Dewi gave a hive of bees to each of his foundations so they would have honey, but they would also have living creatures to care for. The Celts adapted church structures to fit the way they actually lived: the Irish monasteries were tribal, and the Welsh Llans were ideal for caring for scattered rural communities.

ABOVE: The world of fairies.

the clerics beginning to arrive in Ireland from Europe. To his eyes they lacked the ruggedness and the self-discipline of their Irish predecessors. "Silk, satin and featherbeds!" he snorted, "Mitres, rings and chessboards!" How unlike their Irish predecessors of old, "They were not overweight!" The old priests had been roughly dressed, muddy and with wild haircuts, but they were men of keen learning and their natures were pure. They had "very rough monastic rules", which not only order community life, but also encourage self-discipline, without which any spiritual, or mystical, undertaking fails absolutely.

BELOW: The spirit of the night.

SELF-DISCIPLINE

Anyone who aspires to a mystical approach to life must be ready for a radical change of heart, mind and vision. It will have repercussions on both life and lifestyle. New priorities and habits of self-discipline must be acquired. True self-discipline is a gift of grace and must be asked for, as our natural tendency is to take the soft option and settle for the second best. Self-seeking can sometimes be highly motivated and fiercely self-disciplined in the service of self-interest, but mysticism has nothing to do with getting and everything to do with giving of the self, which is never easy.

An Irishman, possibly a priest, wrote angrily of

MYSTICAL EXPERIENCE

*Mysticism, or more correctly mystical experience, is generally understood as direct,
intuitive knowledge of God or ultimate reality, attained through personal experience.*

It is generally recognized that the authenticity of
mystical experience is dependent solely on the quality of life that follows the experience. "By their fruits
ye shall know them," said Jesus, and there are, in any
generation, spurious or pathological "mystical experiences" which are revealed for what they are by the

BELOW: A hermit, extending his faith through learning.

ABOVE: Buddhism stems from mystical experience.

quality of life that follows upon them. Many great
world religions, such as Buddhism and Islam, derive
from the mystical experiences of their founders.

True mystical experience is something that is
given; it cannot be induced and any experiences
which are simply the product of attempts to induce
them are almost certainly bogus. Mysticism is not
about looking for experiences, it is about acquiring
an attitude of heart and mind which sees more profoundly and enters into the wonder and beauty of
creation. It knows creation to be the transfigured
image of the creator. Mysticism is essentially about
learning to love.

ABOVE: Artistic interpretation plays a part in extending the mystical experiences of established religion.

ULTIMATE REALITY

Every world religion has its own distinctive mystical tradition. The direct, intuitive experience of ultimate reality requires to be communicated, for it is never given just for the benefit of the recipient. It is communicated in terms of the language and thought forms of the prevailing culture. True mystics nearly always find that they are closely in tune with each other, whatever their religion. Perhaps the closest and most fruitful dialogue between world religions in recent decades has been that between Christian and Buddhist contemplative monks.

The Celtic tradition is essentially mystical in that it has an innate awareness of the unity of things, of the need for realism, and for an equilibrium between the two human faculties of reason and intuition. In terms of the contemporary Celtic world, some Christian religious traditions are more traditionally Celtic in their approach than others. The Reformed traditions are more rationalistic and tend to be suspicious of intuition, others are more comfortable with it. In any event there should be no confusion between heaven and annwn.

BELOW: St Dwynwen's Cross, Anglesey.

GOD IS LOVE

The Christian experience, expressed in the poetic idiom of doctrine,
is that the Trinity consists of three Persons, not three aspects of the deity.

Examples of triple gods and goddesses are to be found all over the world and even today they exist in aspects of Shivite Hinduism. Celtic paganism was familiar with the idea of triple gods or goddesses, all aspects of the one essential being. To the pagan Celt, therefore, the Christian experience of ultimate reality as a Trinity was not too extraordinary, but the difference is actually profound. The mystery of the Trinity introduces the concept of a personal relationship between three separate individuals. What Christians are saying is that "God is love", but also that God is a love-affair.

LEFT: William Blake's paintings express a personal experience of God.

Celtic Christianity is strongly Trinitarian. The Ortha nan Gaidheal is full of invocations of the Three, and seldom is one mentioned without the others, for God is one and three. God is "The High King of Heaven" and as such may be any or all of the persons. It is the sense of personal relationship within the mystery of Godhead that is the guarantee of divine love, for God could not be love, as St John tells us, were God not first of all a love-affair.

THE RUGGED MYSTICS

Many rocky islets lie just off the west coast of Ireland and on many of them are to be found the remains of a cluster of beehive-shaped stone huts, often surrounded by a dry stone wall. Some of these, put together without mortar, are still almost as their last occupants left them. Some, as on Skellig Michael, appear to cling to a ledge on a bare rock in the middle of the ocean. How could anyone live there?

LEFT: St Kevin's Cell, Glendalough, Ireland.

ABOVE: St Govan's Chapel, Pembrokeshire.

RIGHT: Celtic monastery, Skellig Michael, Co. Kerry.

And who did? They were the Culdees, Christian monks, living a life entirely devoted to prayer. Why? Because they were in love with the love of God.

Here is Celtic mysticism at its most rugged. The Culdees were called to such extremes of self-sacrifice, not just for themselves but for others. They sought to diminish the separation between the spiritual and physical by undergoing spiritual exercises which involved great hardship. It was their part to serve their fellow men and women by holding them before God in prayer and, as far as possible, forgetting all about themselves. There were other hermits, men and women, who lived in gentler places and were also filled with love for God in creation, love of creation and all its creatures in God.

RIGHT: The distinctive beehive-shaped stone huts of the Culdees.

A Mind in the Heart

Mysticism is, first and foremost, an attitude of mind in the heart, and the essential integration of heaven and earth is a reality built into the Celtic vision.

The Celtic mind is revealed both in its pagan past and in its Celtic Christian faith. It is a mind which thinks all things possible. It is possible that heaven and earth are inextricably intertwined. It is possible that there is no essential distinction to be made between the farmer, his cow, the saints and the holy

RIGHT: A holy offering of simple loaves of bread.

angels. It is possible that Bride – once a goddess, now identified with a Christian saint – is a close friend in heaven of the Mother of God. It is possible that the Celtic saints and the holy angels care for mortal men and women and respond, as friends, to their prayers for help. For love, all things are possible.

Because all things are believed to be possible, they are. There is nothing to fear in the old Celtic pagan-ism. Its perversions (such as cruel sacrifice) have been done away with and its insights affirmed and taken up into the true faith. There is nothing to fear because "perfect love casteth out fear" and instead of the past being denied and demonized it has been affirmed and baptized. What might once have been described as superstition, if ever it was, is regarded now as poetry still trying to express the mystery.

LEFT: The Sleeping Earth and the Waking Moon.

RIGHT: Chapel of Our Lady and St Non. St David's, Pembrokeshire.

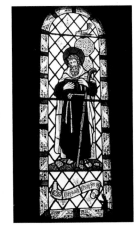

A QUESTION OF ATTITUDE

Mysticism, the attitude of a mind in the heart, is as much as we can aspire to. Celtic tradition can point the way especially to minds that have grown tired with over-full lives, urban stress, noise-pollution and all the mind-pollution that the excessive exposure to the media and modern life in general can induce. Celtic spirituality, or mysticism if you prefer, can be a powerful corrective to the strident, the sickly sentimental and the excessively rationalist, all of which are sometimes to be encountered in contemporary Christianity. Increasingly, those who feel they have lost their way, turn to their roots, and for many these roots are Celtic before they are anything else.

LEFT: Mountain reflected in a dewdrop.

"May the blessing of the rain be on you – the soft sweet rain. May it fall upon your spirit so that all the little flowers may spring up and shed their sweetness on the air. May the blessing of the great rains be on you, that they beat upon your spirit and wash it fair and clean, and leave there many a shining pool where the blue of Heaven shines, and sometimes a star. May the blessing of the Earth be on you – the great round Earth. And now may the Lord bless you, and bless you kindly."
(An old Irish blessing.)

BELOW: Celtic spirituality is radiant with light.

THE FESTIVALS OF THE CELTIC YEAR

The seasons of the year, the solstices, the equinoxes and the cross-quarterings, provided the succession of Celtic festivals, most of which are still celebrated in the calendar of the Christian church. The earth was recognized as a living entity and its cycles were, and still are, reflected in the pattern of human lives, particularly in respect of planting, growth, harvesting and introspection.

Human and animal life begins in the darkness of the womb, so the day traditionally begins at sunset (as, liturgically, it still does) and the Celtic year begins with the coming of the dark.

SAMHAIN, beginning on the eve of 1st November, is a lunar festival and the Celtic new year. It is the time when such cattle as could not be wintered were slaughtered. It is celebrated by the Church as the major feast of All Saints, beginning liturgically

BELOW: Cattle brought down from the hills for winter.

RIGHT: Chopping wood on a medieval farm.

on Hallowe'en, in other words the "eve of all Hallows".

YULE, beginning on the eve of 21 December, is a solar festival when the sun, at its weakest, begins to gather strength. The Yule log is a pre-Christian survival; the Church (until recent revisions) marked Yule with the feast of St Thomas the Apostle. Deep pre-Christian instincts cause Christmas carols to be generally preferred before 25 December (originally the Roman feast of the sun god) rather than after Christmas, as would be liturgically correct.

IMBOLC, the time of the lactation of ewes, is a lunar festival beginning on the eve of 1st February, and is the first day of the Celtic spring. It is celebrated as the feast of St Bride of Kildare and, on 2 February, as the feast of the purification, or the presentation of Christ in the temple.

ABOVE: Resting at harvest time.

OSTARA, the spring equinox and a solar festival, begins on the eve of 21 March. It is closely associated with Lady Day, the feast of the annunciation on the 25th, once celebrated as New Year's Day.

BELTANE, beginning on the eve of 1 May, is the first day of the Celtic summer and an ancient lunar fertility festival, representing the marriage of the complementary powers of masculine and feminine. It is celebrated as the feast of the apostles St Philip and St James.

COANHAIM is the summer solstice, a solar festival, beginning on the eve of 21 June. It is closely associated with the Feast of the Nativity of St John the Baptist on 25 June.

LUGHNASADH, the last lunar festival of the year, begins the season of harvests and hunting. It begins on the eve of 1 August and is traditionally celebrated as Lammas (or loaf-mass) Day, giving thanks for the first fruits of harvest, when the ceremonial first loaf was baked.

HERFEST (from which the word "harvest" probably derives) was the final solar festival of the year, beginning on the eve of 21 September. Harvest homes and thanksgivings are traditional survivals from pagan times and even today are celebrated around the world. The feast of St Matthew, Apostle and Evangelist, is also celebrated on 21 September. The feast of St Michael and All Angels, on 29 September, is also closely associated.

BELOW: Lammas Day, enjoying the first fruits of harvest.

INDEX

animals 38–39, 49

Annwn: Celtic heaven 10–11, 19

  journeying into 24–25

archetypes, meeting the 26

Arthur, King 10, 11, 15, 32

Awen 18, 19, 20, 37

bards 13, 20

Bran the Blessed 31

Bride, Saint see Brigit

Brigit, Saint 34–35, 48–49, 60, 62

Cader Idris 19

cauldrons 18

Celtic background 6–7

Christianity,

  conversion to 32–35

Colmcille 36–37

Columba, Saint see Colmcille

Cuchulainn 15

Culdees 58–59

dance and music 21

David, Saint 39, 54

Dewi Sant see Saint David

druids 13, 20

Earth 10

Earth Mother 30

Fintan 12

geas 19

Gods and Goddesses 30–31

grace 54

Gundestrup cauldron 18, 35

head, cult of the 31

heaven 48–49

  see also Annwn: Celtic heaven

Idris 19

incantations 48, 49

inner silence 22–23

inspiration see Awen

invasions 12–13

Iona 36–37

Ireland 12–13, 33, 36, 55, 58–59

  Irish blessing 61

Lake Bala 11

Llyn Tegid 11

MacCool, Finn 14, 16–17

Mary 34–35, 48–49

Maeve, Queen of

  Connacht 15

manipulation 19

meditation 26–27

Melangell 38–39

Morrighan, the 30–31

music and dance 21

mystical experience 56

nature 21, 23, 44–45

Niav and Oisin 16–17

offerings and prayers 40–41

Oisin and Niav 16–17

ortha 48, 49

Otherworld see Annwn:

  Celtic heaven

paganism 30–31, 58, 60

Patrick, Saint 33

Picts 7

pilgrimages 51

power 19

prayers and offerings 40–41

self-discipline 55

silence see inner silence

sovereignty 20, 30

spirituality 10–11, 46–47, 61

stars 10

Trinity, the 58

Tuatha de Danaan 12–13, 30

ultimate reality 57

warriors 14–15

Yule 62